The Dragon King's Daughter

Written by Charlotte Raby

Illustrated by Alessandra Fusi

Collins

Chapter 1

Hidesato was on a mission. He had to fetch food for his starving brothers and sisters. But a huge white dragon lay across the bridge in front of him, as motionless as any statue. Hidesato looked at it in shock. He knew he couldn't stop now – he had to cross that bridge!

Hidesato strode on to the bridge and faced the dragon.
He was ready to fight.

The dragon blinked; its tail whipped back and forth. Hidesato stepped on to the bridge.

Suddenly, the dragon reared up. An explosion of flames shot from its mouth. Hidesato raised his bow, but in a flash, the dragon disappeared!

"You look so surprised!" chuckled a voice from behind Hidesato. He whipped round and saw a girl in a white kimono.

"I am Princess Biwa," said the girl. "I am the Dragon King's daughter. I can tell you are brave, because you dared to step on to my bridge. I need your help! A giant centipede is threatening the kingdom. Will you help me defeat it?"

Hidesato paused. He knew his family needed him to bring back food. But how could he refuse to help the princess?

Chapter 2

That night, Princess Biwa became a dragon again.
She lay across the bridge. Hidesato followed
the princess's instructions and hid in a tree nearby.

Suddenly, Hidesato felt numb with fear. The giant centipede was crawling in their direction!

The centipede came closer and closer. Hidesato heard its many feet scuttling over the ground.

The dragon stayed as still as a statue.

The centipede took its chance. It rushed forward to attack the dragon.

The dragon blinked, its tail whipped and it vanished.

"Over here!" shouted Princess Biwa to confuse the centipede. Its giant head whipped round. It gnashed its teeth and roared.

"Take that – you big bully!" called Hidesato. He shot three arrows at the centipede.

The centipede staggered backwards. It lost its balance and fell off the bridge, down into the icy waters of the rushing river and away.

Chapter 3

Hidesato climbed on the dragon's back and it flew into the sky. The princess was taking Hidesato to the Dragon King's secret mansion.

They flew over the hills, and then plummeted
down to the sea.

Suddenly, they were diving beneath the waves.
The secret mansion was under the sea!

"Stop!" shouted the servants at the mansion entrance.

Quickly, the dragon turned back into Princess Biwa. "We have an invitation," she said. She and Hidesato went to find the Dragon King.

"Your bravery has helped to save my daughter," said the king to Hidesato. "I have some treasure for you!"

The king unlocked a large treasure chest
and lifted out a golden shield and helmet.
"These are for you," he said to Hidesato.

Then the princess unknotted a shabby-looking bag.

"This magical bag of rice is also for you," she said.
"It will never run out!"

"Thank you, Princess!" exclaimed Hidesato.
He knew his family would never go hungry again!

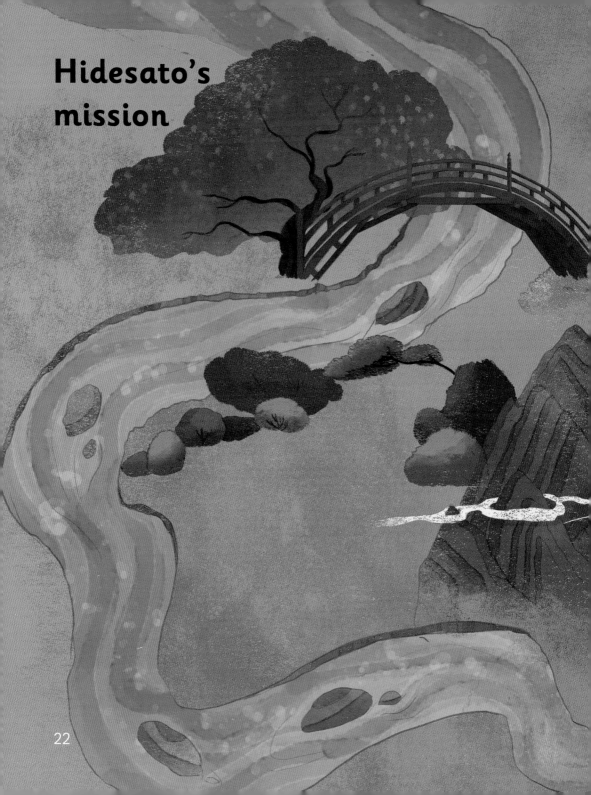

Hidesato's mission

🐾 Review: After reading 🐾

Use your assessment from hearing the children read to choose any GPCs, words or tricky words that need additional practice.

Read 1: Decoding

- Practise reading multi-syllable words. Read the sounds in each syllable (chunk) and blend them. Then blend each syllable to read the whole word.

dis/app/ear/ed	disappeared	ma/gi/cal	magical
cent/i/pede	centipede	scutt/l/ing	scuttling
ex/plo/sion	explosion	mo/tion/less	motionless

- Now read the words quickly without chunking them up.

Read 2: Prosody

- Choose two double page spreads and model reading with expression to the children.
- Ask the children to have a go at reading the same pages with expression.
- Choose some dialogue and discuss with the children how the character might be feeling. Use this to model reading dialogue in such a way as to show emotion.
- Ask the children to choose dialogue and read it in a way that shows emotion.

Read 3: Comprehension

- For every question ask the children how they know the answer. Ask:
  - Can you explain how Hidesato feels at each part of the story, and why?
  - Which character would you like to be, and why?
  - Which word do you think best describes Princess Biwa: clever/resourceful/ quiet? Why?
  - I wonder who was braver. Was it Hidesato or Princess Biwa?
  - Do you think Hidesato's reward was fair?